FANTASTIC FACTS ABOUT

SHARKS

AND OTHER SEA CREATURES

Author
Jason Hook

Editor
Sarah Doughty

Design
Mayer Media

Index
Caroline Hamilton

Editorial Co-ordination
Lynda Lines

This is a Parragon Book
First published in 2000

Parragon, Queen Street House, 4 Queen Street, Bath BA1 1HE, UK

Produced by Monkey Puzzle Media Ltd
Gissing's Farm, Fressingfield, Suffolk IP21 5SH, UK

ISBN 0-75253-167-0

Printed in Italy

FANTASTIC FACTS ABOUT

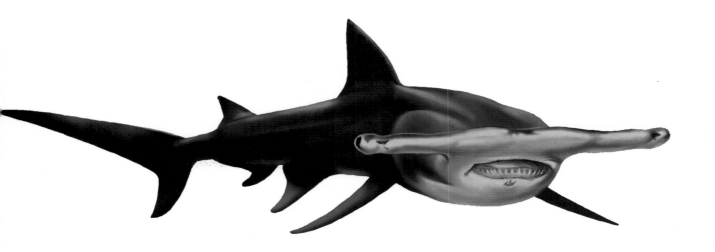

SHARKS
AND OTHER SEA CREATURES

p

CONTENTS

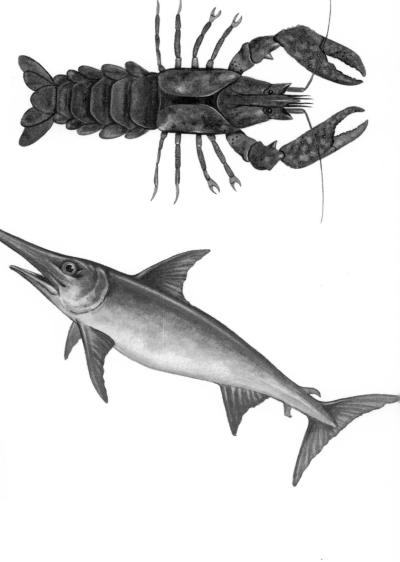

SHARKS

The sea covers 71 per cent of the Earth's surface, and is so deep in places that Mount Everest could be submerged within it. This enormous underwater world contains amazing communities of creatures, each one adapted to the light, heat and habitat of its home. Vertically the oceans can be divided by depth and light – stretching down through the sunlit zone, twilight zone, dark zone and abyss, to the blackness of trenches over 6,000 metres (19,700 feet) deep. Horizontally, habitats include coastlines, reefs and open oceans of different climates. In nearly every region and at every depth lives some form of shark.

NURSE SHARK
The nurse shark is also found in tropical waters, but it lives on the sea-bed. It grows to about 4 metres (13 feet) long. It has wide, flattened teeth for crushing the lobsters, crabs and snails it finds there to eat.

The nurse shark has these protrusions, or barbels, above its mouth which help it detect prey buried under the sand.

TIGER SHARK
The tiger shark is typical of most people's idea of a shark. It is a fast, dangerous hunter which cruises over tropical reefs. Adults can reach over 6 metres (20 feet) in length and will attack humans. The tiger shark has serrated teeth, shaped like its own dorsal fin, which can cut through the bodies of the turtles, seals, large fish and the young birds it feeds on.

Sharks belong to a family of fish called elasmobranches, a word which comes from the Greek for "beaten metal" and "gills". Unlike most fish, which have a skeleton of bone, the shark's framework is made of cartilage. This is a light, flexible substance – which is in fact, as tough as beaten metal. It forms the shark's hard, thick fins, which are different from the delicate, spiny fins of most fish. Like all fish, sharks have gills for extracting oxygen from the water, but unlike a fish, a shark's gills have no such covering.

Tigers and nurses
- In 350 BC, the Greek writer Aristotle noted one main feature of sharks: "Of those fish that are provided with gills, some have coverings for this organ, whereas all the selachians [sharks] have the organ unprotected by a cover."

- The tiger shark has been recorded as devouring animals and people – cattle, donkeys and pigs and unfortunate people that have fallen from ships. When tiger sharks have been captured and examined, shoes, petrol cans and number-plates have been found in their bellies.

- In April 1935, a tiger shark was caught alive off New South Wales, Australia. It coughed up a tattooed human arm. Discovering the arm had been cut off, rather than bitten off by the shark, it became the evidence in a murder investigation.

- The nurse shark can roll up its pectoral fins beneath its body to form a tunnel. When a lobster mistakes this tunnel for a safe crevice in the reef, it crawls into its last ever hiding place!

TYPES OF SHARK

There are about 370 species of shark, and they come in all shapes and sizes. Whale sharks and basking sharks are the largest. Then there are the ferocious predators like the great white, tiger and hammerhead, which cruise over huge areas hunting for prey. Smaller species, like angel sharks and dogfish, live on the sea-bed near coasts and on reefs. The smallest, like the pygmy shark and lantern shark, dwell in the dark abyss below 3,500 metres (11,500 feet). There may be some sharks we have never seen. The most recent discovery was a deep-sea shark called "megamouth", which was caught in 1976 when one swallowed a ship's anchor.

HAMMERHEAD
Some sharks have the most amazing appearance. A hammerhead's wide head is thought to contain sensors which help it detect its prey. It can also use its head rather like an aeroplane's tail, tilting it up and down to change the angle of its movement. It feeds on other sharks, but has a particular taste for stingrays – which it pins down with its strange head before biting.

DOGFISH

The commonest sharks found in European waters are the various species of dogfish. These are small and harmless – not many people's idea of a shark at all. Dogfish nuzzle around muddy bays, feeding on crustaceans and worms. Females spawn eggs in cases which they attach to sea plants by curly strings. Old egg cases which are found washed up on beaches are known as "mermaids' purses".

The angel shark looks more like a ray, but like all sharks, its gills are behind its eyes – a ray has them beneath its fins.

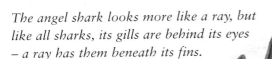

Whoppers and tiddlers

- The whale shark is the largest of all fish. It reaches over 14 metres (45 feet) long, and weighs up to 15 tonnes (15 tons). That is over three times the length of an African elephant and over twice as heavy. They are able to grow to such huge proportions because their bodies are supported by water.

- The whale shark is not normally dangerous to humans. However, it has been known to ram fishing boats – it may have mistaken the boat for another shark or was too busy swimming and feeding to notice it.

- The smallest sharks are the lantern sharks and the dwarf or pygmy sharks, which grow to only some 20 centimetres (8 inches) long – 70 times smaller than the whale shark.

ANGEL SHARK

Sharks which live on the sea-bed, like the wobbegong, nurse shark and this angel shark, have flattened bodies and excellent camouflage. They lie hidden waiting for their prey. The angel shark has large pectoral fins, rather like an angel's wings. When fish or squid swim overhead, a terrifying transformation takes place. Suddenly, its pancake body rears up, and its enormous mouth engulfs its victim.

9

A PERFECT DESIGN

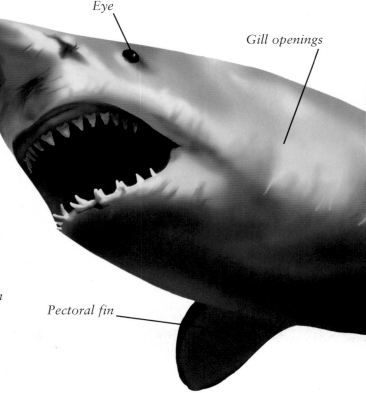

The shark's hearing is acute, it has excellent vision in darkness and its sense of smell is more developed than that of any other fish. The shark also has a "lateral line system" of fluid-filled canals along the sides of its body, which can sense injured prey disturbing the water. Sensors on the shark's snout called *ampullae of Lorenzini* can even locate a fish hiding beneath the sandy sea-bed from the tiny electric fields produced by its gills. It is impossible to hide from this perfect predator.

BUILT FOR SPEED
With a head shaped like a bullet and a powerful, streamlined body, sharks such as the great white shown here can accelerate very quickly. A warming system heats the shark's muscles for greater energy, and side-to-side movements of the shark's tail create a powerful thrust. A shark's skin is surprisingly rough, with small, tooth-like scales which reduce water resistance.

Unlike other fish, sharks have no gill covers to pump water over their gills. Instead, by swimming they force water into their mouth and out through their gill slits. This is known as "ram-jet ventilation". Sharks also lack the gas-filled "swim bladder" of other fish. They have a large liver filled with oil which gives some buoyancy, but sharks must swim constantly to stay afloat.

Eye

Gill openings

Snout

Pectoral fin

GREAT WHITE BITE

Sharks have up to 3,000 teeth in their mouths, arranged in rows. As a tooth in the front rows becomes blunt, one from behind moves forward in a "conveyor belt" system to replace it. So, a shark's teeth are always sharp. The great white has triangular, serrated teeth which can bite lumps out of whales and seals. This fearless predator attacks with a "bite and spit" action. It takes a single massive bite, then – to avoid injury – retreats until its victim has bled to death.

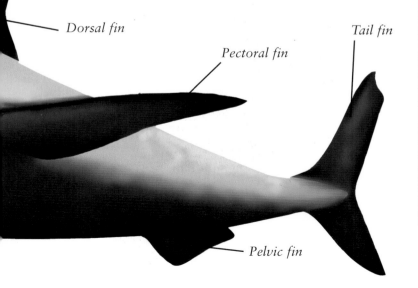

Dorsal fin

Pectoral fin

Tail fin

Pelvic fin

Shark facts

- A shark's jaws can exert 300 times more pressure than a human's. The force of a dusky shark bite has been measured at 3 tonnes/cm² (20 tons/inch²), but no one has yet dared to measure that of the great white. The great white detaches its upper jaw from its skull to allow it to take a massive bite out of its victim.

- A shark's skin is rough, but its ability to slip through water has been studied by the designers of yacht keels. Dried sharkskin, called shagreen, was once used as sandpaper.

- Because of the way it replaces blunt teeth, a shark may use 20,000 teeth in its lifetime.

- A shark can smell one drop of human blood in 100 million drops of water.

- A dogfish has the greatest sensitivity to electric fields in the animal kingdom. Using its *ampullae of Lorenzini*, it can sense an electric field 25 million times weaker than one which a human could detect.

11

ATTACK AND DEFENCE

Sharks are very difficult to observe, and the way they hunt remains something of a mystery. Many, such as the great white, are solitary hunters. Hammerheads also hunt alone at night, but during the day large numbers of them congregate in sinister schools. Deep sea lantern sharks hunt in packs, which surround and herd their prey. Only sharks of a similar size swim together, because big sharks regard their smaller relatives as an attractive meal.

A large or bloody prey, such as a dying whale, will attract a crowd of hungry sharks. In this case, a "feeding frenzy" sometimes develops, in which the sharks will attack anything that moves – including each other.

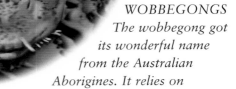

WOBBEGONGS
The wobbegong got its wonderful name from the Australian Aborigines. It relies on camouflage for attack and defence. The wobbegong is also called a carpet shark, and looks like an ancient, frayed rug. Its mottled brown, grey and yellow markings blend with the colours of the sea-bed. It also has incredible, raggedy flaps of skin hanging from its jaws as if it has just swallowed seaweed. Its prey mistake it for a weed-covered rock. Unlike the white shark, the wobbegong is not normally aggressive – unless you happen to tread on one!

Their ferocity is perhaps the most frightening feature of the shark. Fishermen hunting whales claim to have cut the guts out of a shark and thrown them back into the water. The shark, injured but not dead, came back to attack whales tied alongside the ship.

GREAT WHITE HUNTER

The great white is the one creature in the sea which fears nothing – except perhaps a larger great white. It grows to over 6 metres (19 feet) and weighs over 2 tonnes (2 tons) – over 25 times the weight of an average human. The great white hunts by stalking its prey, slowly circling below its victim. Then it suddenly accelerates towards the surface. During the attack, the great white's eyes actually retract into their sockets for protection. The great white's markings are a form of camouflage, allowing it to attack unseen. Seen from below, its white belly blends with the sky. From above, its dark back blends with the shadows of the sea's depths.

Special abilities

- The thresher shark has the longest fin of any fish, a tail up to 3 metres (10 feet) long. It uses this fearsome weapon to herd schools of small fish and stun them so that it can devour them.

- When a swellshark feels threatened, it swallows water and swells its bumpy body up like a balloon, so that it can wedge itself safely in a crevice, away from danger.

- The great white shark has specially adapted eyes to help it adapt to its environment. It has a mirror at the back of its eyes called a tapetum. This reflector doubles the amount of light the shark has to see by in the dark depths. The great white also has a curtain of coloured cells which protect its eyes in brighter light, rather like sunglasses. In shallow waters it can shade just the top half of its eye, so that it can see well into the brightness above it and into the darkness below it!

13

DIET

All sharks are meat eaters, with a diet of fish, molluscs and crustaceans. Sharks also eat each other. One Greenland shark caught through an ice-hole had swallowed a shark of almost equal size to itself, up to its head. Examining the stomachs of captured sharks has revealed the head of a crocodile, a whole reindeer, plastic bags and broken clocks. If it eats something it doesn't like, a shark can practise "gastric eversion". The shark turns its stomach inside out and pushes it through its mouth. When the unwelcome or poisonous meal has been violently ejected, the stomach is sucked back in again.

TASTY TURTLE
Turtles are just one of the many specials on the tiger shark's menu. It will eat seals, whales, sea birds, large fish and carrion such as dead dogs. Tiger sharks also devour poisonous jellyfish and sea snakes, and seem immune to their venom.

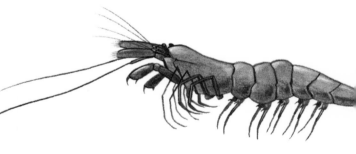

CRUSHED CRUSTACEANS
Sharks which live on the sea-bed eat crustaceans like this lobster, as well as octopus and small fish. Horn sharks have a combination of small, sharp front teeth for clutching crustaceans, and broad, blunt back teeth for crushing their shells.

The biggest shark, the whale shark, actually eats the smallest prey. Like the basking shark and megamouth, this gentle giant is a "filter feeder". These sharks use their enormous mouths to gulp in over a million litres (220,000 gallons) of water each hour as they swim, like giant vacuum cleaners. With tiny teeth and sponges in their throat and gills, they filter out the millions of microscopic creatures called plankton on which they live.

Cookie-cutters
- For many years, fishermen were puzzled to see fish, whales and seals with perfect circles cut out of their flesh. Underground cables and the dome of a nuclear submarine were also found to have these neat incisions. They come from the cookie-cutter shark – a thin, brown shark only about 50 centimetres (20 inches) long, also known as the cigar shark. The cookie-cutter has extendible jaws and large lips like a sucker, which it uses to attach itself firmly to its victim. It then twists its body around like a can-opener, using its razor-sharp lower teeth to cut out a perfect plug of flesh. The cookie-cutter can make itself glow in the dark, which it probably does to lure its prey close enough for it to attach itself.

SEAL MEAL
The great white shark has a particular taste for seals and sea lions, which it has been known to swallow whole. It will attack dangerous elephant seals. It will also devour dolphins, penguins and other sharks, such as the beautifully coloured leopard shark. The great white is the most feared man eater. Its attacks on humans may result from the similar silhouette and movements of a swimmer and seal when seen from below.

15

SHARKS AND HUMANS

 As the biggest and most ferocious fish, it is not surprising that tales of the shark appear in the myths of coastal peoples. In Tahiti and Fiji, sea gods take the form of sharks. The Haida, a people of North America, carve pictures of sharks into their totem poles. In one Hawaiian myth, villagers notice that a stranger called Kapa'aheo is absent every time swimmers are attacked by a shark.

MAN EATERS
There are about 50 shark attacks on people every year. The great white is the most feared man eater, but nearly 30 other species have attacked people. The four most dangerous are the great white, tiger, bull and oceanic white tip sharks. Sharks are attracted to wounded prey, just like any predator. After air and sea disasters, blood in the water will lure crowds of sharks and stir up a feeding frenzy. Great whites will occasionally launch unprovoked attacks, and can only be safely observed from cages.

When they finally fight off the shark with spears, the stranger dies. He is transformed into a shark-sized column of rock, which can still be seen in Honolulu.

Tales of ferocity have not stopped people hunting the shark for its skin, teeth and fins. The Inuits of the Arctic made rope from the skin of the Greenland shark, and knives from its teeth. The Maoris of New Zealand wore the teeth of the mako shark as earrings. Millions of sharks are killed each year, caught in the drift nets of fishermen or in mesh set up to protect beaches. In China, shark-fin soup is an expensive delicacy. Fishermen often remove the fins while the shark is still alive, then throw away the rest of the carcass. Today, many sharks are threatened species.

Shark attacks

- In 500 BC, the famous Greek historian, Herodotus, wrote of sharks attacking shipwrecked Persian sailors. Five hundred years later, the Roman writer Pliny described sharks menacing Mediterranean sponge divers.

- Most sharks live in seas rather than rivers. But attacks on humans have been recorded in rivers, too. In both the River Ganges in India and over 200 kilometres (125 miles) up the Limpopo River in Africa, there have been shark attacks on humans.

- During the Second World War, American sailors and pilots who had to ditch in the water were advised to thrash about to scare away sharks. Unfortunately, this is exactly the sort of behaviour which attracts sharks. In 1942, the troopship *Nova Scotia* was sunk off South Africa. A thousand men were lost, many killed by sharks.

- In South Africa, December 1957 is known as Black December, because of shark attacks. In December and the months that followed, five people were killed by sharks south of Durban. After this, nets were put up to protect the beaches.

17

FISH

Sharks are related to two groups of fish – rays and chimaeras. All three groups have skeletons of cartilage. Rays are the sharks' closest cousins, even though they look very different. Most have very flat bodies with gills underneath, and huge pectoral fins like wings. They swim by making rippling movements with their fins, like giant birds flying gracefully through the water. There are over 450 species of ray, including guitarfish, sawfish and skate. Many rays, such as the stingray, have sharp, poisonous spines on their tail. These are not always effective in fighting off sharks – one hammerhead was found with nearly 100 stingray spines in its mouth. The torpedo ray has a more convincing defence – it can produce an electric shock of some 200 volts. This is like a shock from domestic house wiring.

Cephalic fins (either side of mouth)

Five pairs of huge gills

Diamond-shaped disc (the combination of pectoral fins, head and body is called the disc)

Thin, whip-like tails (the manta ray has no sting)

MANTA RAY
The manta is three times wider than the height of a man, and it can weigh over 1,300 kilograms (590 pounds). Manta is Spanish for blanket and these creatures look like huge magic carpets sweeping through the ocean. They gently harvest plankton, just like the whale and basking shark. On either side of its mouth, the manta ray has special fins which it uses to usher the plankton inside. They can leap 5 metres (16 feet) out of the water to dislodge parasites from their bodies.

CHIMAERAS

Like sharks, chimaeras have a skeleton of cartilage and no swim bladder. Unlike sharks, they have gill covers and their skin is smooth. There are three types of chimaera. Short-nosed chimaeras like this ratfish have mouse-like faces and long, thin tails. Ploughnose chimaeras or elephantfish have a flared trunk which points downwards. Longnose chimaeras or spookfish have a sharp, upturned snout.

Evolution

- Sharks, rays and chimaeras are related because they evolved from common ancestors. The earliest sharks appeared 400 million years ago, 200 million years before dinosaurs and over 390 million years before humans.

- Chimaeras started evolving from sharks about 340 million years ago. Rays did not develop until some 140 million years later. They probably evolved from sharks with flat bodies. The first rays may have been similar to today's sawfish and guitarfish. These look like sharks, but have their gills on their undersides like all rays.

- The frilled shark looks like a type of shark called the *Cladoselache* which lived 350 million years ago. The deep-sea frilled shark has ruffled skin over its gills, which gives it a "frilly" collar. It looks more like an eel, and has three-pronged teeth like a dinner fork.

- Teeth have been found from the *Carcharodon megalodon*, an ancestor of the great white shark which lived 25 million years ago. Imagine meeting one – it was like a great white but 15 metres (50 feet) long and weighing 25,000 kilograms (11,400 pounds). Scary!

BONY FISH

There are over 14,000 species of marine fish sharing the sharks' underwater empire. Most of them belong to a group known as "bony fish". Unlike the cartilage skeleton of the shark, their skeletons are made from bone. Bony fish come in a fantastic array of shapes and rainbow colours. There are parrotfish with beaks like birds, unicornfish with extraordinary noses, and butterfly fish decorated in psychedelic patterns. To the shark, bony fish are a vital food source. In the ocean "food chain", plankton is eaten by small fish, who are eaten by bigger fish, who are in turn eaten by many sharks.

OAR FISH
The oar fish is the world's longest bony fish, and can grow to almost the same length as a whale shark. It looks like a snake with a flame-red mane, and is probably the creature that sailors once described as a sea serpent. The smallest fish is the Philippino dwarf pygmy goby, which at an average length of 8 mm (⅓ inch), is nearly 2,000 times smaller than a whale shark.

OCEAN SUNFISH
Most sharks give birth to a small number of live young, called pups. Most bony fish, though, give birth to large numbers of eggs. The ocean sunfish produces the most – nearly 30 million in one go. The sunfish grows up to 4 metres (15 feet) long, and often basks on the surface like an enormous silver plate.

DRUMFISH

Many people imagine that the underwater world is a silent place. In fact, sound travels well in water and the seas echo with songs, squeaks, clicks and rattles. Some fish, like the sunfish, make noises by grinding their teeth. This drumfish makes a drumming noise by vibrating its swim-bladder.

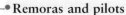

Remoras and pilots

- A shark has some strange fish as friends. Fish called remoras have dorsal fins which look like the soles of training shoes. They use these as suckers to attach themselves to a shark. A whale shark sometimes looks as if it has a beard because so many remoras are attached around its huge mouth. Remoras act as cleaners, eating parasites which live on the shark. They also detach themselves to feast on scraps from the shark's meal.

- Sharks are also pursued by annoying companions called pilot fish. They feed on scraps left over from the shark's feasts, and are protected from predators who avoid the shark. Other fish, such as king angelfish and barberfish, act as cleaners, eating parasites from the skin of the shark.

- Blennies act as cleaner fish for large fish like groupers and snappers. But the sabretooth or false-cleaner blenny, when approached by a fish seeking a good grooming, will rush in and bite it instead.

OCEAN PREDATORS

A family of large bony fish called billfishes look much more like sharks than rays do, even though they are not related. This family of ocean cruisers includes marlin, sailfish and spearfish. Their most striking feature is a long upper jaw or bill, shaped like a spear. Swordfish also have this weapon – but it is flattened like a sword. All these fish have a lot in common with predator sharks. They are fierce hunters and meat eaters, preying on schools of fish. They have the same body-shape and large, sickle-shaped tail as the faster sharks, and can reach even greater speeds. They also have the same type of camouflage. Their dark backs blend with the sea when seen from above, but their pale bellies are camouflaged when fish below them look up into the sunlight.

SWORDFISH

Swordfish can grow to 6 metres (20 feet) and weigh 0.5 tonnes (0.5 ton). They are solitary fish, like the great white shark. Their famous sword-like snout is rough, like the skin of a shark. It cuts into the water to help the swordfish swim faster, and is used as a weapon to slash at schools of fish. Swordfish swords are sometimes found broken off, inside the bodies of whales. They have also been known to pierce the keels of ships, causing them to spring a leak.

SAILFISH

The sailfish is the fastest swimmer of all fish. It has a powerful tail, and a distinctive, spotted purple dorsal fin like a yacht's ragged sail. It can fold this fin into a groove on its back to increase streamlining – turning it into a smoother, faster torpedo. Like a sail, the dorsal fin can be raised again at slower speeds. The sailfish also uses it as a barrier to prevent the fish it is feeding on from escaping.

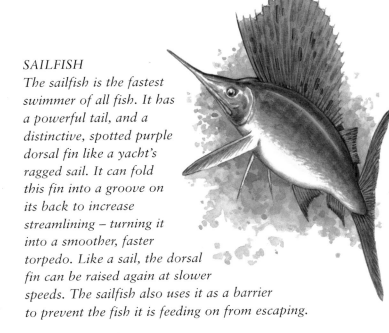

BLUE MARLIN

Marlin hunt in packs to herd fish like mackerel into tight, frightened schools. These hunters then enjoy a fine feast. They slash around with their bills to herd and stun their victims as they feed. A marlin enjoys eating so much that it changes colour when feeding, with parts of its body glowing a dazzling blue.

Snouts and sprinters

Swordfish and billfish closely resemble a number of unusual sharks and rays:

- the goblin shark, which has a long, paddle-shaped snout used for detecting prey
- the sawshark, which has a snout resembling the blade of a chainsaw, with teeth sticking out from the sides of it
- the sawfish, a type of ray, which has a similar snout to the sawshark and uses it to slash at fish and to dislodge crustaceans and molluscs from the sea-bed.

Sharks and billfish are among the fastest swimmers in the ocean:

- sailfish have demonstrated speeds of 110 kph (68 mph) – over 15 times faster than a person could manage
- the short-finned mako shark is the gold-medal sprinter among sharks. It is one of the only sharks fast enough to hunt and catch swordfish. It has a very similar shaped tail to billfish, with top and bottom halves of similar size.

23

TWILIGHT TORCHES

Between depths of 200 and 1,000 metres (650–3,250 feet) is the twilight zone. Only a small amount of sunlight penetrates this deep, so the bony fish found here live in permanent dusk. Consequently, they need their own torches. Life at this depth is like a miniature laser show. Fish like the viperfish, hatchetfish, dragonfish and midshipman have organs which produce light. They use this light to lure or illuminate prey, and to camouflage themselves. Lanternsharks, pygmy sharks and cookie-cutters can all produce light along their undersides.

VIPERFISH
The viperfish has a row of organs called photophores which produce jewels of light along its body. There are 300 more minute lights inside its mouth. It also has a lure extending from its dorsal fin, on which hangs a light shaped like a worm. It seems the viperfish can adjust its array of lights so that only this lure is seen. When prey are drawn toward the lure, the viperfish impales them on its enormous fangs. This is quite a light show when you consider the viperfish is only 30 centimetres (11 inches) long.

Lure

Fangs

Luminous mouth

Light organs

Light organs

Large eyes

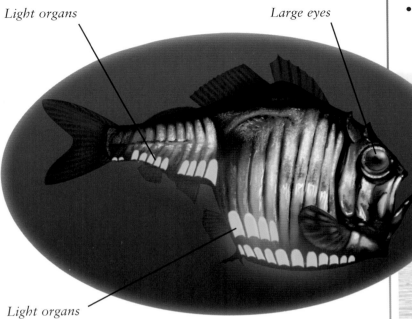

Light organs

HATCHETFISH

The hatchetfish has a hatchet-shaped body with scales like silver foil. Its enormous eyes give it excellent vision in the twilight. A hatchetfish spends its days in twilight, then at night ascends to shallower waters where there is more food. It will travel 500 metres (1,640 feet) up and down in 24 hours. This puts enormous pressure on its swim-bladder, because the gas in it expands nearer the surface. It is able to release this gas, like a hot-air balloon. The hatchetfish produces light from photophores on its underside which enable it to drop down on prey unseen.

Producing light

- Light produced by living organisms such as fish and fireflies is called bioluminescence.

- The flashlight or lanterneye fish produces light from tubes filled with luminous bacteria. It cannot control the brightness, so it has a mechanism for covering up the light so that it flashes on and off like a torch. The light can be seen from 30 metres (100 feet) away.

- Many fish have complex organs called photophores, and can control the amount of light they produce. The midshipman fish has 840 photophores in its belly.

- In the deep sea, normal rules of vision do not apply. Fish actually use their lights to hide themselves! Just as a shark's white belly makes it hard to see from below, so deep-sea fish light up their undersides to blend with the faint sunlight from above. Even at 1,000 metres (3,250 feet), a fish would have a slight silhouette when seen from below, but the weak glow of the photophores makes them invisible.

25

DEEP SEA ANGLERS

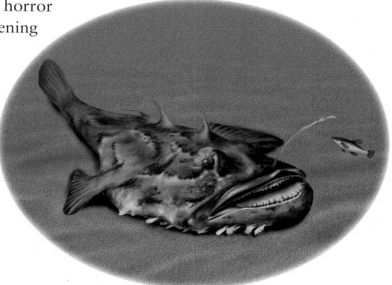

Beneath the twilight zone lies the last unexplored part of the Earth. It is a pitch black world deeper than the Grand Canyon, where temperatures fall below 4 °C (39.2°F). At first sight, the bony fish which live there look like monsters from a horror film. In fact, they are less frightening than they seem. Because food is scarce, most deep-sea fish grow to only a few centimetres long. Their ferocious-looking teeth are brittle. Their soft, jelly-like bodies are "pressurized" to resist the enormous weight of water above them. If they were brought too quickly to the surface, they would explode!

A FULL STOMACH

Anglerfish have incredibly elastic stomachs, which will stretch to fit in almost any meal. An anglerfish measuring 9 centimetres-(3.5 inches-) long was found with its stomach containing an eel, a hatchet fish, a bristlemouth and five shrimps. A good night's fishing!

FOOTBALL FISH: FOLDAWAY TEETH

The anglerfish looks like an old, torn leather football. It has small eyes, because eyesight is not important in its darkened world. Because food is rare, anglerfish have to be able to eat whatever comes their way. Their needle-sharp teeth fold back to allow them to swallow prey much bigger than themselves. They make the most of each meal, digesting it extremely slowly.

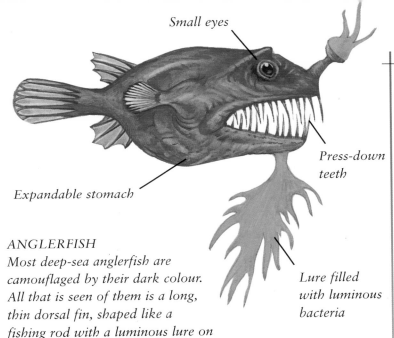

Small eyes

Press-down teeth

Expandable stomach

Lure filled with luminous bacteria

ANGLERFISH

Most deep-sea anglerfish are camouflaged by their dark colour. All that is seen of them is a long, thin dorsal fin, shaped like a fishing rod with a luminous lure on the end. Rather than waste precious energy chasing fish, they wait like patient fishermen for this lure to attract their prey. When a victim comes close enough, the angler sucks it into its mouth. Sharks also use lures: the megamouth has a luminous mouth, so that reflections from the crustaceans it swallows will lure others into its jaws.

True Love

- A number of species of anglerfish have a very unusual way of mating. The male is some 20 times smaller than the female. He connects himself to his much larger mate by biting her anywhere on her body. The male then becomes a parasite. His mouth becomes joined to her skin, and their blood streams are connected. He becomes completely dependent upon his mate. She is responsible for finding enough prey to feed them both. In effect, the two anglerfish become a single creature containing both sexes. His only function is to fertilize her eggs. Such a creature is called a hermaphrodite. Is this true love? Only for the male. Females are often found with several little husbands attached!

TRIPODFISH

Another deep-sea fisherman is the tripodfish. It has long strands stretching from the base of its tail and pelvic fins, which it uses to stand on the sea-bed like a telescope on a tripod. From here, it extends long feelers up into the current to detect prey.

MUDSKIPPERS

We saw how the prehistoric *Cladoselache* evolved over millions of years into modern sharks. A more amazing evolution was the way fish developed into amphibians. The first amphibians were simply fish who learnt to survive out of water. They had to develop lungs and their fins became limbs. Today, there are fish called mudskippers who survive on muddy shores when the tide goes out.

MUDSKIPPER

The mudskipper's short pectoral fins look like a frog's feet. It uses them to scuttle across the mud and even as adhesive suckers for climbing. On land, the mudskipper also faces the problem of keeping its bulging eyes moist. It has a thick layer of transparent skin to protect them, and can roll the eyes back into their sockets to moisten them. Some mudskippers protect their eyes from bright sunlight with a dark pigment – rather like putting on sunglasses.

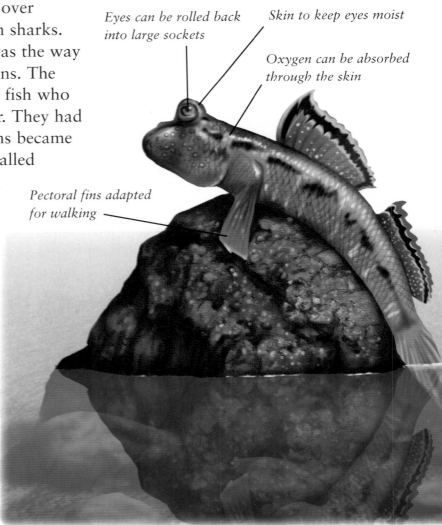

Eyes can be rolled back into large sockets

Skin to keep eyes moist

Oxygen can be absorbed through the skin

Pectoral fins adapted for walking

They have to overcome the same problems their prehistoric ancestors faced: how to breathe and move. The evolution of fish into amphibians is even more important when you think that amphibians evolved into humans. How does it feel to be related to a mudskipper?

Walking fish

• Mudskippers can jump as well as walk. By curling up their bodies and straightening them suddenly, they can flip themselves up to 60 centimetres (24 inches) through the air. Mudskippers will chase each other across land, and can also scamper across the surface of the water.

• Eels can slither across land like the snakes they resemble. They use the same wriggling movements as when they swim.

• Some sharks which dwell on the sea-bed, such as carpetsharks, have such strong pectoral fins that they can crawl along the ocean floor. Fish called gurnards can also dance along the sea-bed using the three spines at the front of their pectoral fins.

MONTAGU'S BLENNY
Not all blennies live in mud. Montagu's blenny lives in rockpools. When it becomes stranded at low tide, it seems able to map a route back to the safety of the sea. It will scurry from rockpool to rockpool, until it finds itself back in the ocean.

All fish, including sharks, breathe with their gills. As water passes over the gills, oxygen is absorbed from the water into the fish's blood. Underwater, mudskippers breathe in this way. When the tide goes out, they have other ways of breathing. Just as divers carry tanks of oxygen, so the mudskipper stores water inside its gills to supply oxygen. It can also extract oxygen from the air through its thin skin. Finally, it can increase its oxygen levels by gulping in air.

29

FLATFISH

The bodies of rays and sharks like the angel shark are flat from top to bottom, as though they have been squashed by something pressing down on them. Flatfish, such as the plaice and flounder, are different – their bodies are flattened sideways. They look as if they have been run over by a steamroller while lying on their sides. The way they become flatfish is incredible. They start off shaped like ordinary fish. As they grow, the body becomes flattened. Next, one eye moves or "migrates" to join the eye on the other side of the head! At first, the fish is blind on one side. But then the adult flatfish settles on the sea-bed. It spends the rest of its life on the sea-bed, and can watch for prey above it with both eyes. Its side has become its top! It has

PLAICE
Some flatfish have their eyes on their left side, and some on the right. Left-eyed flatfish include turbots, brills, topknots and megrims. Right-eyed species include plaice, halibuts and soles. Flounders can be either. Because the mouth does not move round, the migration of their eyes can make the face of a flatfish look very twisted. The brown and orange markings of this plaice camouflage it on the sea-bed. Its underside is white – it needs no camouflage because it is rarely seen.

become a flatfish. The whole process, in the case of a common sole, takes about 35 days.

FLOUNDER

Flounders can change colour to blend in with their backgrounds like chameleons. They are the best make-up artists in the ocean, and can become almost invisible. If they are laid on a chessboard, they can imitate its black-and-white squares. This right-eyed flounder has made itself sand-coloured to match the colour of the sea-bed. Its flat body helps to hide it. Many flatfish wriggle into the sand to further disguise themselves, leaving only two eyes sticking up.

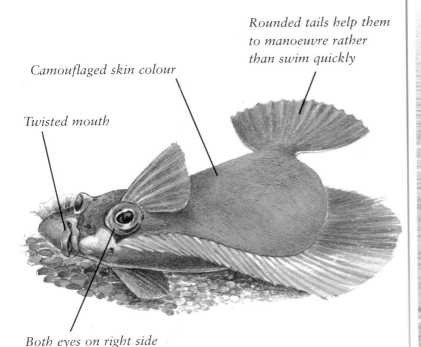

Rounded tails help them to manoeuvre rather than swim quickly

Camouflaged skin colour

Twisted mouth

Both eyes on right side

Camouflage

- The scales of a fish are transparent, but its skin contains cells called chromatophores which provide colour. By filling these cells with different levels of pigment, many fish can change colour.

- Whole shoals of pale fish can vanish among coral by having silver skin and a simple black stripe to break up their shape.

- Stonefish allow weed and anemones to grow on their skin to further disguise their body, which is already brilliantly camouflaged. The tasselled wobbegong shark has similarly camouflaged skin and weedy fringes to hide it. The bramble shark has spikes on its skin like thorns, which are also a form of disguise.

- Beautifully coloured butterfly fish have a black band across the eye to disguise it, and a large spot on their tail which looks like an eye. If a predator attacks this false eye, the butterfly fish is more likely to survive. They add to this camouflage by swimming backwards!

31

DIFFICULT PREY

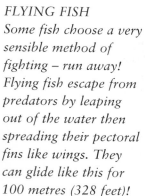

In many cases, the ocean food chain is based on bigger fish eating smaller fish. But this is not always how things work. There are certain fish with special methods of attack and defence which make them much more dangerous than you would imagine. The colour of a fish is not just used for camouflage. Some brightly coloured fish are just warning other members of their community that if they attack them, they are in for a very nasty surprise.

The hidden spine at the base of the tail is used as a blade.

SURGEONFISH
Brightly coloured surgeonfish have a concealed spine on their tail which they can extend like a flick-knife. It is as sharp as a surgeon's scalpel and contains poison. It is a lethal defence against predators when the surgeonfish lashes its tail at them.

FLYING FISH
Some fish choose a very sensible method of fighting – run away! Flying fish escape from predators by leaping out of the water then spreading their pectoral fins like wings. They can glide like this for 100 metres (328 feet)!

PORCUPINE FISH

When it is swimming around normally, the porcupine fish looks quite ordinary. It is yellow and black, and has spines flattened against its body. When it is attacked, however, it sucks in water – just like the swellshark. This expands its body to three times its normal size. That is enough to scare away most predators. But when the porcupine fish swells up, its spines also stick straight out. It turns into a giant pincushion which would be very uncomfortable when stuck in the throat of any fish foolish enough to swallow it.

Spines stand erect when the porcupine fish is inflated

Bright colours warn of danger

Poison

- The Moses sole found in the Red Sea squirts a poison from its dorsal and anal fins which repels sharks. Sharks are unable to close their mouth around this poisonous sole.

- The pufferfish of the Indo-Pacific and Red Sea is the world's most poisonous fish. It contains a poison in its ovaries, blood, liver, intestines and skin. Less than 0.1 gramme (1/300 ounce) of this poison would kill a person in under 5 minutes. Like the porcupine fish, the puffer swells up when threatened.

- The Greenland shark found beneath the ice of the Arctic has a special defence – poisonous flesh. Dogs which have eaten the flesh of Greenland sharks caught by Inuit fishermen stagger around as if they were drunk.

- Weever fish bury themselves in sand with poisonous spines sticking up from their backs.

INVERTEBRATES

One thing that sharks and other fish have in common with us is that they have a backbone. All creatures with backbones – including humans and other mammals, birds, reptiles, amphibians and fish – are called vertebrates. There are about 40,000 species of vertebrates.

But there are over a million species of creatures without backbones, called invertebrates. Over 160,000 of these species are sea creatures. They include molluscs such as squid and octopus; jellyfish and anemones; corals and starfish; and crustaceans like lobsters and crabs. While they may appear harmless, many are hunters and predators, just like sharks and fish, fighting a miniature war for survival.

SUN STAR

Although they look harmless, starfish are actually quite scary creepy-crawlies. Their tops are protected by spines. The undersides of their arms have hundreds of tiny, suckered "tube-feet". They waggle these to and fro to scamper along the sea-bed like a centipede. This sun star preys on other starfish, but many starfish feed on mussels or oysters. They attack by grasping the two halves of the oyster's shell with their suckers, and pulling until the oyster becomes exhausted. When the oyster opens a crack, the starfish turns its stomach inside out through the mouth at its centre. It presses the stomach into the oyster, and begins to digest its flesh before even swallowing it!

CUSHION STAR

Starfish are a more advanced invertebrate than jellyfish. They belong to a group called echinoderms, which means spiny-skinned. There are over 2,000 types of starfish. Most have five arms, like this cushion or bat starfish. But some have up to 40. Unlike most creatures, starfish have no obvious front or rear end, no left or right. They are happy moving in any direction.

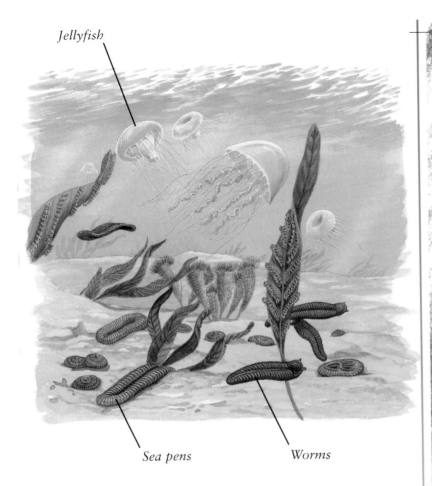

Jellyfish

Sea pens

Worms

SIMPLE INVERTEBRATES

Some invertebrates evolved over 500 million years ago, a long time before the first sharks. They have very simple bodies. The jellyfish which look like parachutes have a hollow pouch with a mouth surrounded by tentacles. The sea pens, which look like plants, are actually animals which catch tiny creatures as they drift past. The creatures that look like slugs are worms, of which there are many types in the sea.

Investigating invertebrates

- One square metre (3 feet square) of mud taken from the sea-bed off the coast of Holland contained 4.5 million marine nematode worms. There are enough of these creatures in the world to form a layer around the entire world!

- Because water supports their bodies, marine invertebrates can grow much larger than those on land. The largest sea invertebrate, the giant squid, can grow to over five times the size of the biggest land invertebrate, the giant earthworm.

- Invertebrates have amazing abilities, just like sharks and fish. The crown-of-thorns starfish is covered with sharp, poisonous spines to defend itself against predators. It feeds on the animals which form corals. Plagues of these starfish can devour an entire coral reef – they have become a major environmental problem.

- A starfish has the ability to "regenerate" itself. If one of its arms is cut off, it simply grows back a new one. Very handy.

OCTOPUSES AND SQUIDS

With their grasping tentacles and staring eyes, squids and octopuses have a special place in the gallery of sea monsters. The terrifying Kraken which attacks ships in Norse myths, was probably based on giant squids seen by Norwegian sailors. The Atlantic giant squid is the largest of all invertebrates, and can measure over 15 metres (49 feet) from head to the tips of tentacles.

Squids and octopuses belong to a family of molluscs called cephalopods. They are the most intelligent invertebrates, and their eyes have a similar biology to those of humans. A squid's ten tentacles and an octopus's eight will each grow back – like a lizard's tail – if bitten off.

Both squids and octopuses are "jet-propelled". They swim by sucking water into their bag-like body or "mantle", then blasting it out through a funnel.

ARMED AND DANGEROUS
The octopus lurks in crevices, camouflaging its skin with muscles which contract or expand cells of different colours. The octopus jets after crabs and clams, then drops on them like a parachute. It grasps its victim with suckered tentacles so agile that they can unscrew bottletops. Then it kills with a sharp beak which contains poisonous saliva. This little blue-ringed octopus is the most poisonous of all molluscs, holding enough poison to kill ten humans. When angry, it displays incredible, electric-blue markings.

STREAMLINED SQUID

Squid have perfect streamlined bodies to help them glide through the water. They use their tentacles – with suckers – to catch their food and their fins are used for pushing them forwards. If they want to move quickly they squirt water from a funnel behind their head which propels them forwards.

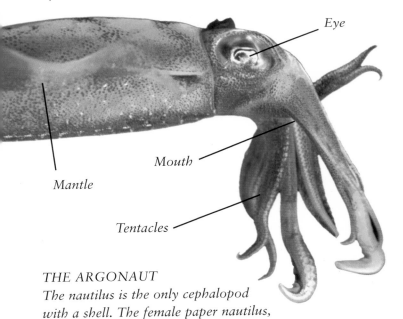

Eye

Mouth

Mantle

Tentacles

THE ARGONAUT

The nautilus is the only cephalopod with a shell. The female paper nautilus, shown here, releases a liquid which hardens into the paper-thin shell where she stores her eggs. The paper nautilus is also known as the argonaut. It was named after the ship Argo, sailed by Jason in Greek mythology, because the Greeks believed the nautilus moved by using two of its arms as sails and two more as oars.

Squid Facts

- The biggest giant squid ever discovered had a body 6.1 metres (20 feet) long, and tentacles stretching over 6 kilometres (4 miles). It was washed ashore in Newfoundland in 1878.

- "Flying squids" can launch themselves out of the sea and glide through the air for 30 metres (98 feet) to avoid predators. The vampire squid lives up to 5 kilometres (3 miles) below the surface and swims not with a jet but with cloaked or webbed arms. The sail squid can light up spots on its body, like a firefly. It has one eye four times larger than the other.

Octopus Facts

- In 1866, the popular Victor Hugo novel *The Toilers of the Sea* portrayed the octopus as a terrible monster and made it the talk of Paris. Hats in the shape of octopuses became popular with fashionable women.

- Some octopuses in captivity have eaten their own arms (probably due to stress) – which then grew back!

37

OTHER MOLLUSCS

 There are nearly 100,000 species of molluscs. As well as squid and octopus, they include gastropods such as snails, limpets, whelks and slugs; and bivalves such as clams, mussels and oysters. Mollusc means "soft-bodied", and most of these creatures have a body like a jelly protected by a hard shell. Most of them live on the sea-bed, and creep across it on a single foot. The octopus's eight arms are simply divisions of this foot. Most molluscs have a mantle, like the octopus. Many also have a radula, a tongue covered with teeth. These teeth gradually move forward to replace those that are worn out, just like the teeth of a shark.

SEA HARE

You are what you eat, especially if you are a gastropod called a sea hare. The sea hare changes colour to match the plant it is eating – red if it is grazing on red algae, green if it is eating green algae. So, it is always camouflaged when having its dinner. It has one other colourful defence. It can shoot out purple ink when alarmed.

DOG WHELK

Some meat-eating gastropods are determined hunters. The dog whelk has a rough snout or proboscis, which it uses to file a hole into the shell of a mussel or the cement of a barnacle. It then uses its toothed radula to scrape up and consume the delicious soft flesh inside. Other gastropods, such as the necklace shell, speed up the drilling process by dripping acid on to their victim!

SLIPPER LIMPET

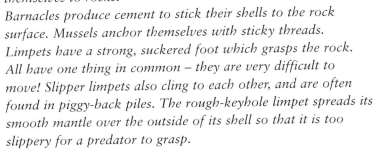

Many molluscs find protection by withdrawing inside their shells and attaching themselves to rocks. Barnacles produce cement to stick their shells to the rock surface. Mussels anchor themselves with sticky threads. Limpets have a strong, suckered foot which grasps the rock. All have one thing in common – they are very difficult to move! Slipper limpets also cling to each other, and are often found in piggy-back piles. The rough-keyhole limpet spreads its smooth mantle over the outside of its shell so that it is too slippery for a predator to grasp.

The molluscs' armoury

- Clown sea slugs have no shell, so they have an unusual type of defence. They simply do not taste very nice, and have brightly coloured spots advertising this fact to passing predators.

- Cone shells have teeth which they can fire like harpoons into fish or worms. These teeth contain nerve poison which will paralyze quite large fish. The poison of the geographer and tulip cones has been known to kill people.

- Some sea slugs use borrowed weapons. They feed on jellyfish and anemones with poisonous stings. When the sea slug digests these stings, it regrows them through its own back. It can then use them as a "second-hand" defence.

- A starfish trying to prise open a scallop can sometimes get a nasty surprise. The scallop can flap the two halves of its shell to squeeze water out of its mantle and make a jet-propelled escape – rushing past the startled starfish!

JELLYFISH

 You might think that a shark is much more dangerous than a jellyfish. But jellyfish have killed more people than all the great whites put together. Jellyfish are related to anemones and corals. They all belong to a group of invertebrates called cnidarians. This means "nettle animals", but many of these creatures possess stings far more dangerous than any nettle. Ninety-six per cent of a jellyfish is made of water, so it floats very easily. As it drifts and swims through the oceans, it stings to death any fish or crustaceans which collide with its tentacles.

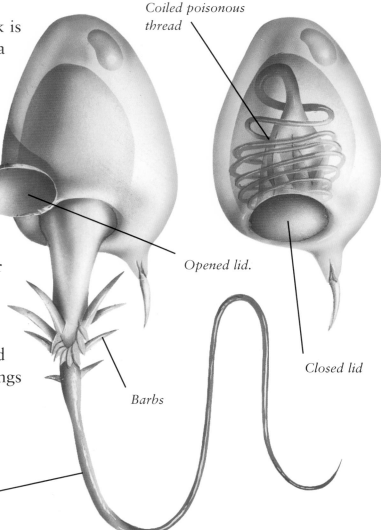

Coiled poisonous thread

Opened lid.

Closed lid

Barbs

Released poisonous thread

INSIDE A JELLYFISH

A jellyfish has a simple body made of two layers. The outer layer or bell contains the muscles used for swimming. The inner layer is mostly a stomach or gut. The two layers are separated by a jelly-like substance which forms a sort of skeleton and gives the jellyfish its name. At the bottom is a ragged curtain of "oral arms" which funnel food up into the jellyfish's stomach. The fringe of tentacles sting prey or trap them with a sticky fluid.

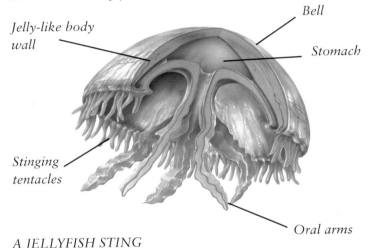

Bell

Stomach

Jelly-like body wall

Stinging tentacles

Oral arms

A JELLYFISH STING

Jellyfish do not attack, they just wait for their prey to collide with them. Their tentacles are like a drifting minefield. Every tentacle has millions of little mines in it called nematocysts. Each mine is filled with a barbed, poisonous thread, coiled up like a spring and held down by a lid. When a chemical triggers the mine, it releases the lid. The miniature mine explodes, and the barbed and poisonous threads are fired into their victim. The powerful poison stops the prey's heart, and the thread holds it like a harpoon. After use, each nematocyst is absorbed into the jellyfish's body and replaced by a new weapon.

The jellyfish armoury

- At least 65 people have been killed by box jellyfish in the last 100 years. In Queensland, Australia, in 1943, a number of troops were killed by these jellyfish during military exercises.

- The most venomous snake, the taipan, has enough venom to kill 30 people, who would take several hours to die. The box jellyfish has enough poison in its tentacles to kill 60 people. Its poison is powerful enough to kill somebody in three minutes.

- Atolla jellyfish are made of jelly as tough as rubber. They are red, but if attacked will glow a luminous blue. Some jellyfish will shed a luminous tentacle if alarmed, to try to distract their attacker.

- Turtles can eat poisonous jellyfish. They are immune to their stings.

- Jellyfish come in some very attractive colours. Some are pale white, but many are fabulous shades of yellow, orange, pink or red.

JELLYFISH COMMUNITIES

Most jellyfish start their lives as little tubes called "polyps" anchored to the ocean floor. These polyps form into buds, which float off into the sea. They develop into the adult jellyfish form, which is called a "medusa". The jellyfish now turns into a floating community. Hundreds of baby crabs hitch a ride on its bell while they grow. Other crustaceans called isopods set up home inside the body of the jellyfish, stealing the food it catches. Fish like jacks and medusafish seem immune to the jellyfish's sting. They use its tentacles as a harbour, safe from predators. It is thought that they do not release the chemical which makes the jellyfish release its poisonous stingers.

BOX JELLYFISH
The jellyfish can swim by expanding its bag-like outer body, then squeezing it together to force out water. This jet-propulsion makes the jellyfish ascend. It then drops down gently like a parachute, eating anything caught by its tentacles.

SEA WASP
The box jellyfish, which has quite a square bell, is one of the most poisonous creatures in the world. It is also called a sea wasp, because it can inflict millions of tiny stings. Its body is the size of a football and it can have up to 60 tentacles. Swimmers often fail to see it, because it is almost transparent and its tentacles are only a few millimetres thick.

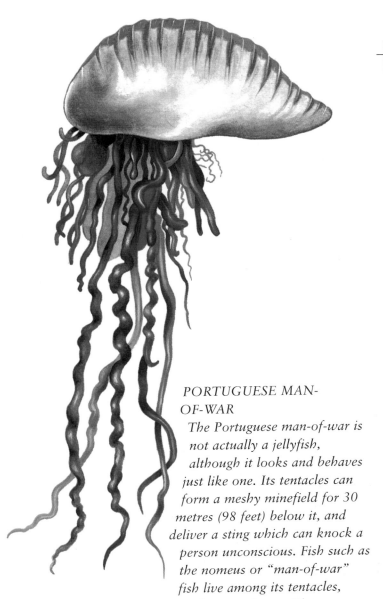

PORTUGUESE MAN-OF-WAR

The Portuguese man-of-war is not actually a jellyfish, although it looks and behaves just like one. Its tentacles can form a meshy minefield for 30 metres (98 feet) below it, and deliver a sting which can knock a person unconscious. Fish such as the nomeus or "man-of-war" fish live among its tentacles, using them as protection from predators. They seem able to avoid its sting most of the time, although the man-of-war does occasionally eat them!

A ship with many sailors

- The Portuguese man-of-war got its name because sailors thought it looked like a type of ship called a man-of-war. It is quite an unusual jellyfish. It is made up of hundreds of different creatures called polyps, all joined together like the parts of a single ship! This type of "collective" animal is called a siphonophore.

- There are four types of polyp forming the Portuguese man-of-war. One polyp forms a living sail, which keeps the rest of the "ship" afloat. It fills itself with air and drifts along just above the surface of the water. Every now and again, it lets out the air and dips under the water to keep itself moist. Below the "sail" polyp is the ship's "rigging" – each tentacle is a separate polyp whose job is to sting prey. They pass any food they capture up to the third type of polyp, whose job is to digest food. The fourth type of polyp is in charge of the reproduction of the Portuguese man-of-war.

SEA ANEMOMES

 Sea anemones come from the same family of cnidarians as jellyfish. But they do not look much like them. This is because an anemone's body is like an upside-down version of the jellyfish. They have a simple body or stalk shaped like a sweet packet, but the mouth and tentacles are at the top rather than hanging down. This form of creature is called a polyp. A sea anemone can creep along the sea-bed, but most of the time it cements its foot to rocks by producing a form of glue.

Sea anemones are named after woodland flowers. They may look like flowers, but in fact they are another meat-eating hunter, fighting the underwater battle for survival. Any passing fish, shrimp or worm that strays too close to a sea anemone will be engulfed by its tentacles, poisoned and passed to the central mouth to be consumed.

Stinging tentacles

Mouth

DAHLIA ANEMONE
If you turn this picture upside down, you can see how similar anemones really are to jellyfish. Their mouth is located at the top of the body at the centre of a ring of tentacles, which sting using exactly the same poisonous nematocyst "mines" as the jellyfish. Some anemones actually fight duels with each other! They inflate bundles of nematocysts and wave them at an anemone that is invading their space. The biggest anemone usually wins!

Stalk or column

Adhesive base

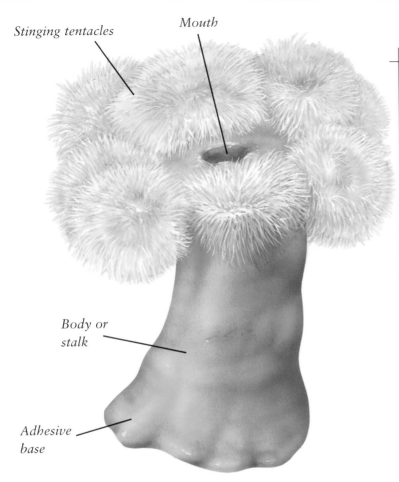

Stinging tentacles

Mouth

Body or stalk

Adhesive base

PLUMOSE ANEMONE

This plumose anemone feeds on food particles drifting past in the water, which it catches with up to 200 tentacles. Plumose means "feathered", which describes the way its tentacles look. The anemone has few enemies. The bright colours of its tentacles warn predators that it is poisonous and does not taste very nice. Sea slugs, though, are immune to the anemone's poison, and will happily try to gobble one up. If a sea slug attacks, or if the tide goes out, the sea anemone withdraws all its tentacles and shrinks into a hard, shiny ball.

Living in harmony

• Anemones and clownfish have a relationship similar to that of sharks and remoras. An anemone's tentacles normally inject a poisonous sting into anything that touches them, but clownfish are immune. They have a thick slime or mucus covering their body, and it does not contain the chemical which triggers the anemone's harpoons. When a family of clownfish first choose an anemone for their lodgings, they further protect their bodies by gently rubbing against the anemone. This coats the fish with the anemone's own mucus. The anemone then provides a home safe from intruders, where the clownfish can lay their eggs beneath a burglar alarm of stinging tentacles! Sometimes clownfish nip their host to make it spread its tentacles over the nest. The anemone also gets something in return from the clownfish. The fish attract other kinds of fish for it to eat and always defend their chosen anemone ferociously – a bit like a guard dog.

CORALS

You probably know that many sea creatures – including the wobbegong, tiger shark and various reef sharks – live on coral reefs. But did you know that the coral itself is a sea creature? Like the Portuguese man-of-war, a coral is really a colony of many tiny polyps, all working together. Each polyp extracts calcium from the water, which it uses to build itself a limestone tower. A colony of polyps joins their towers together into a single castle. Layers of living tissue, like secret underground passages, join all the polyps together. Neighbouring colonies of polyps build their own castles, and a living, underwater city is created. When polyps die, new polyps build their own towers on top of them. A living city grows up on top of the skeleton of the old one, and the coral reef continues to grow.

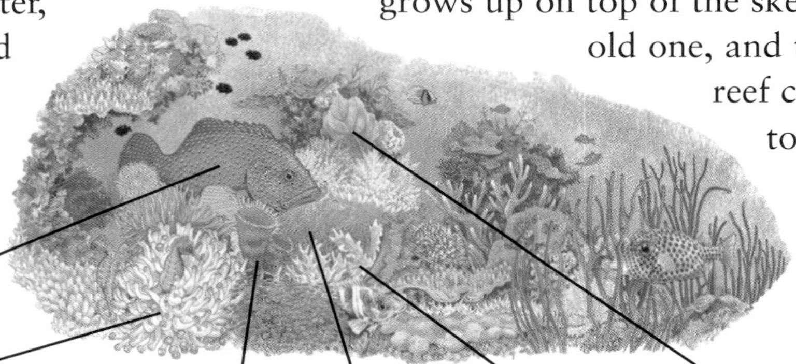

Coral grouper

Anemone

Sponge

Brain coral

Fire coral

Sea fan

CORAL REEF
Different types of coral build their castles in different shapes. Brain corals grow in curving rows, creating a coral castle which looks just like a human brain. Organ-pipe corals build towers like little tubes, which look like the pipes of a church organ.

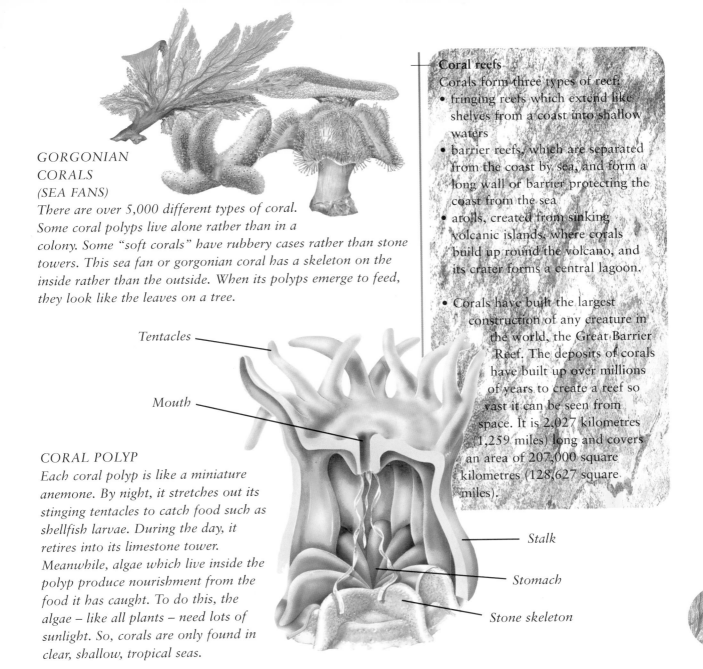

GORGONIAN CORALS
(SEA FANS)

There are over 5,000 different types of coral.
Some coral polyps live alone rather than in a
colony. Some "soft corals" have rubbery cases rather than stone
towers. This sea fan or gorgonian coral has a skeleton on the
inside rather than the outside. When its polyps emerge to feed,
they look like the leaves on a tree.

Tentacles

Mouth

CORAL POLYP

Each coral polyp is like a miniature
anemone. By night, it stretches out its
stinging tentacles to catch food such as
shellfish larvae. During the day, it
retires into its limestone tower.
Meanwhile, algae which live inside the
polyp produce nourishment from the
food it has caught. To do this, the
algae – like all plants – need lots of
sunlight. So, corals are only found in
clear, shallow, tropical seas.

Stalk

Stomach

Stone skeleton

Coral reefs
Corals form three types of reef:
- fringing reefs which extend like shelves from a coast into shallow waters
- barrier reefs, which are separated from the coast by sea, and form a long wall or barrier protecting the coast from the sea
- atolls, created from sinking volcanic islands, where corals build up round the volcano, and its crater forms a central lagoon.

- Corals have built the largest construction of any creature in the world, the Great Barrier Reef. The deposits of corals have built up over millions of years to create a reef so vast it can be seen from space. It is 2,027 kilometres (1,259 miles) long and covers an area of 207,000 square kilometres (128,627 square miles).

47

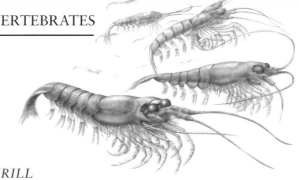

CRUSTACEANS

Over three-quarters of the world's animals belong to a group of invertebrates called arthropods. As well as insects, this group includes crustaceans such as barnacles, crabs, crayfish, krill, lobster and shrimp. Like insects, crustaceans have segmented bodies divided into a head, thorax and abdomen; and pairs of jointed legs. A hard shell protects their soft bodies. Most live and hunt on the sea-bed. Krill, though, drift on the currents, where they are an important food source.

KRILL

Near the surface of the oceans drift clouds of organisms called plankton. They include microscopic plants (phytoplankton) and tiny animals (zooplankton). Phytoplankton are eaten by zooplankton, who are eaten by fish, who are eaten by sharks and dolphins. Among the zooplankton are millions of tiny, luminous crustaceans called krill. One swarm of krill seen off Antarctica was estimated to weigh 10 million tonnes. It is a good job that there are so many krill, because the biggest fish (whale sharks) and the biggest mammals (blue whales) miss out the other links in this food chain and feed directly on them.

SPINY LOBSTERS

Lobsters are among the largest crustaceans, and can live for 100 years. When storms approach in autumn, these spiny lobsters migrate from coral reefs to deeper waters in an incredibly orderly manner. The lobsters line up single-file, with each lobster touching its antennae to the tail of the lobster in front. Up to 100,000 of them then march for 80 kilometres (50 miles) in perfect queues of up to 70 lobsters each!

BARNACLES

Although they are crustaceans, many barnacles feed in a similar way to anemones. They attach their shells to rocks, then wave their feathery feet in the water to collect food. Clever barnacles, though, are the hitch-hikers of the underwater world. They attach themselves to whales, and let the whales carry them through clouds of delicious plankton. Barnacles also attach themselves to the keels of ships, in such numbers that they slow the ship down. They sometimes get a taste of their own medicine. These goose barnacles attach themselves to acorn barnacles which have attached themselves to a whale!

Sound waves

• The fastest gun, or rather the loudest gun, in the sea is surely the pistol shrimp. It is only 5 centimetres (2 inches) long, but it has an enormous front claw. The pistol shrimp "fires" this claw by snapping two parts of it together – like a pair of castanets. It does this so hard that the noise can shatter glass and set off alarms on navy submarines. When the shrimp fires its "pistol" at fish, they are knocked unconscious by the sound waves it makes. The shrimp then quietly devours them.

• Spiny lobsters have a scraper at the bottom of their antennae which they rub against their foreheads. This makes a rasping sound which can be heard 50 metres (164 feet) away. The lobsters feed on the sea-bed in packs of as many as 1,000. When a hungry shark approaches, they rub their scrapers to sound the alarm and warn each other of the hungry predator!

CRABS

As the favourite food of many sharks, crabs need strong defences. They do not build stone castles like coral, but are equipped with a suit of armour or shell, called a carapace. Most of the 4,500 different species of crabs are meat eaters. They hunt down other crustaceans, scavenge for dead creatures on the sea-bed or eat tiny organisms in the water. Armour is not the crab's only defence. Soldier crabs can burrow into the sand like a corkscrew to hide. Ghost crabs are extremely fast runners. Crabs can also detach a leg if a predator grasps it, allowing the crab to limp to safety – where the leg will grow back.

CRAB
A crab has five pairs of legs. The front pair has pincers for fighting and eating. The other legs are used for walking, which the crab does sideways. When a crab grows, its armoured carapace does not. So it has to be thrown away regularly. In a process known as "moulting", the crab detaches its muscles from the old shell and breaks out of it. The crab often eats its old shell. It then hides until its new, soft shell has hardened.

Pincer or chela

Antennae

Eyes on stalks

Shell or carapace

Ischium

Merus

Propodus

Dactylus

Base of abdomen

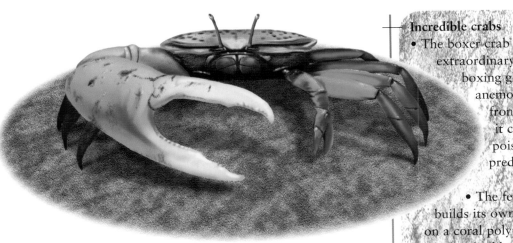

FIDDLER CRAB

The male fiddler crab has one pincer much bigger than the other, which it waves about to attract a female. It also uses the claw to arm-wrestle with other males. When the fiddler is eating, it uses the larger claw as a knife to smash the shells of snails or oysters, and the daintier claw as the fork to pass meat into its mouth.

HERMIT CRAB

Hermit crabs do not grow their own carapace. They live in the old shells of sea snails. When they grow too big they look for a new home, often trying to evict each other from nicer shells. Many hermit crabs decorate their mobile homes with sea anemones. The sea anemone gets free transport, while the crab gets a poisonous burglar alarm. When it moves to a new shell, the hermit crab drums its pincers on the anemone until it moves with it.

Incredible crabs

- The boxer crab wears an extraordinary pair of flowery boxing gloves. It holds an anemone in each of its front two claws so that it can throw a poisonous punch at predators or prey.

- The female coral gall crab builds its own prison. It settles on a coral polyp and waits for the coral to build a limestone tower around it. The crab becomes totally enclosed, apart from small pores for food to be passed in, and for the much smaller male to enter.

- Decorator crabs cover their shells with sponges and anemones for camouflage and protection. They have hundreds of tiny hooks on their shell to hold their disguise in place. The tiny pea crab actually lives within the shell of a mussel, and steals its food from there.

51

REPTILES

Reptiles may have scaly bodies, but few of them live in the ocean. Marine iguanas and saltwater crocodiles are part-time visitors. But the only reptiles who live in the ocean full-time are sea turtles and sea snakes. They do not have gills like sharks and fish, and have to surface to breathe. But they have developed the hunting skills to survive. Sea snakes have lungs stretching the length of their bodies, and can stay underwater for two hours. They are poisonous, and can quickly subdue dangerous and slippery prey like eels. The beaked sea snake contains enough venom to kill 53 people. Sea snakes can also swallow prey much bigger than themselves. Sometimes two snakes swallow the opposite ends of a large fish. But the smaller snake usually joins the fish on the menu!

GREEN TURTLE
The green turtle is the most common turtle. Unlike most reptiles, it is a vegetarian. It is the fastest turtle, and uses its flippers in a flying motion, like a big, leathery bird. It can reach speeds of nearly 32 kph (20 mph). Turtles need to swim well because females will travel over 2,000 kilometres (1,243 miles) to sites where they can lay their eggs.

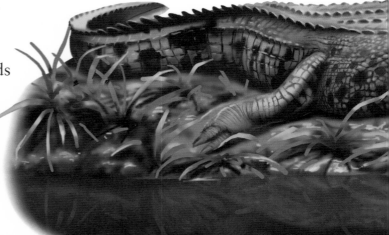

LEATHERBACK TURTLE

The leatherback is the largest sea turtle. It can grow to almost twice the length of a person, and weigh over 500 kilograms (1,100 pounds). It gets its name because its shell is covered in a leathery coat rather than scales. Like all turtles it is vulnerable to sharks, because it cannot withdraw its flippers all the way into its shell.

SALTWATER CROCODILE

The saltwater crocodile is the largest living reptile. It grows to 8 metres (26 feet) long and can weigh over 1,000 kilograms (2,200 pounds). This deadly reptile will eat sharks, turtles, birds, cattle and humans. It is far more dangerous than the great white shark. On average, 2,000 people a year are thought to be killed by saltwater crocodiles. On the night of 19 February 1945, Allied soldiers trapped over 800 Japanese troops in a coastal swamp on Ramree Island off Burma's coast. By the following morning, saltwater crocodiles had eaten all but 20 of them!

The fight to survive

• In November every two or three years, green turtles living off the Brazilian coast make an eight-week, 2,000 kilometres (1,242 miles) journey to Ascension Island. The female drags herself ashore at night. She uses her flippers to scrape a hole, then lays over 100 eggs and covers them with sand. She makes great sighing noises, and the glands that she has to remove excess salt make her cry saltwater tears.

• The eggs hatch after two months. All the babies face a hard battle for survival. They have to work together to dig themselves free. They are attacked immediately by hungry ghost crabs, monitor lizards and sea birds. They head for the brightest light – the open sea. Entering the water, they are preyed upon by fish like snappers and groupers, then by sharks and tuna. Those few females which survive will eventually return to lay their own eggs.

53

MAMMALS

 Most mammals, like reptiles, are happier on dry land. The typical features of a mammal's life are not suited to an underwater existence: they breathe air, need a steady body temperature and give birth to live young. Only a few groups have adapted to life at sea. Whales have mastered their ocean home completely, and are its largest residents. Though they are mammals, they never leave the sea. The dugong and manatee also spend their whole lives in the water. Seals, sea lions and walruses are magnificent underwater hunters, but they rarely travel far from shore.

DUGONG

The dugong and manatee are the only plant-eating mammals in the sea – they are sometimes called sea cows. The dugong uses its squashed, bristly snout and short flippers to uproot grasses from the sea-bed. It is a slow, gentle creature, which stays in shallow waters to avoid predators like sharks. Females, with their sad faces and habit of sitting upright in the water to nurse their young, were mistaken by sailors for mermaids.

SEA OTTER

The sea otter is the smallest marine mammal, and the only one with no blubber. It keeps warm with a "life-jacket" of air trapped beneath its fur – which is the thickest of any mammal. Sea otters live near the shore, but spend most of their lives afloat on beds of seaweed called kelp. At night, they wrap themselves in kelp sleeping bags, and let the ocean rock them to sleep. Sea otters are skilled tool-users. Floating on their backs on the surface, they often rest a stone on their bellies and use this homemade anvil to smash open the shellfish they have caught.

CRABEATER SEAL

Seals, sea lions and walruses have fur coats and a layer of blubber to keep them warm underwater. With streamlined bodies and powerful flippers, they are brilliant swimmers who dive for fish and shellfish. The southern elephant seal can dive to an incredible 1,700 metres (5,578 feet) and stay underwater for two hours. It spends 90 per cent of its life at sea. All seals come ashore to moult and breed on remote islands safe from predators. The crabeater seal is the most common, with a population of over 10 million.

Memorable mammals

• Apart from whales, the elephant seal is the largest mammal. It can weigh over 4 tonnes (4 tons), which is more than a female African elephant.

• The most dangerous seal is the leopard seal of the Antarctic. It will attack and eat penguins, and has been known to chase humans across the ice – but probably only because it has mistaken them for a delicious emperor penguin!

• In 1768, Steller's sea cow, an enormous relative of the manatee and dugong which weighed about five times more than them, was made extinct by human hunters.

• Sea otters have to digest food very quickly, which helps to keep them warm. But it means they have to hunt and eat constantly, and consume three times as many calories as a person.

WHALES

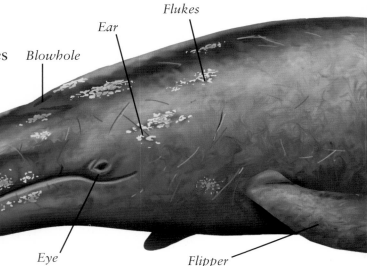

Blowhole
Ear
Flukes
Eye
Flipper

Whales, dolphins and porpoises belong to a group of mammals called cetaceans, which means "sea monsters". They are called monsters only because some whales are incredibly big. The blue whale is the largest creature ever to live on this planet, but it is a gentle creature. Most mammals are not suited to life underwater, but whales live there as successfully as sharks and fish. Until 1758, scientists thought whales were fish, but there are some important differences. A shark has gills for breathing underwater, but a whale has lungs and has to surface to breathe. A shark has a tail with fins on the top and bottom, and swims by swishing it from side to side. The whale's tail, though, has fins on each side, and moves up and down.

GREY WHALE

All whales have a rounded body, which grows thinner from front to back. They are brilliantly streamlined, with few fins to drag in the water. Most whales have a dorsal fin, but this grey whale just has a ridge. Apart from the tail, the only fins are two flippers at the front, used for steering. The tail has large, flat horizontal fins called flukes, which propel the whale's enormous body through the water. When it surfaces, the whale breathes out through its blowhole.

BLUE WHALE

The largest dinosaurs weighed as much as 15 elephants, but the biggest blue whale weighed 190 tonnes (190 tons)– as much as 38 elephants. A newborn blue whale weighs up to 3 tonnes (3 tons), growing into a 26-tonne- (26-ton-) baby by the age of one year. Whales can grow so much bigger than mammals on land because their bodies are supported by water. There is also so much food in the sea. As they evolved over millions of years, blue whales got bigger because the biggest ones survived better in the ocean. It is frightening to think blue whales may still be evolving, and could be even bigger in a million years time!

Wonderful whales

- The beluga is a beautiful white whale, which looks like it has been carved out of snow. Its colour may offer camouflage, because it lives in the Arctic. It is the only whale which can change the expression on its face.

- With their long, thin jaws, beaked whales look like enormous dolphins. But they have a pair of large teeth sticking out from their bottom jaw. A male strap-toothed beaked whale has bottom teeth which curve so far around its top jaw that it cannot open its mouth properly.

- The blue whale can blast a cloud of stale air up to 9 metres (30 feet) from its blow-hole. A whale's spout is visible because the air it breathes out contains droplets of water and oil.

NARWHAL

One of the strangest whales is the narwhal of the Arctic. The male has a magnificent spiral tusk sticking out from its head, which it uses to fence with other males. The myth of the unicorn was probably based on a narwhal.

57

WHALE BEHAVIOUR

Whales can be divided into two groups – baleen whales and toothed whales. There are 11 species of baleen whales, including the blue, grey, humpback and right whales. They are all "filter-feeders" like the whale shark. They have a material called baleen in their mouths which sieves plankton and fish out of the water. There are 67 species of toothed whales, which include the sperm and pilot whales, dolphins, porpoises, beluga and narwhal. They are all predators who hunt for fish, squid and other prey. They have a single nostril in their blowhole, while the baleen whales have two.

GREY WHALE
The grey whale is a baleen whale, but it has its own way of feeding. It dives to the bottom of the sea, and dredges up mouthfuls of mud. The grey whale forces this mud through its baleen plates, and sifts out molluscs, crustaceans and worms.

BLUE WHALE

Baleen whales swim near the surface, where they feed on clouds of plankton, krill and fish. They have hundreds of plates hanging down the sides of their mouths – made from baleen – a material similar to our fingernails. The plates are covered with thick hairs. The whales take huge gulps of water, then squeeze it out through the plates at the sides of their mouths. The hairs on the baleen plates allow water to pass, but trap any food. The blue whale and other "rorqual" whales like the humpback and minke have a flexible throat which can balloon out into an enormous scoop. They fill this with enormous quantities of water when feeding. Their prey may be tiny, but the blue whale can consume 4 tonnes (4 tons) a day.

SPERM WHALE

Toothed whales dive deep for their food. Unlike seals, they dive with their lungs full of air. Below 100 metres (328 feet), their lungs collapse but their blood keeps up the oxygen supply. The sperm whale is the biggest toothed whale, and the champion diver. Humans normally breathe 15 times every minute at rest, and can hold their breath for three minutes. The sperm whale breathes 4 times a minute at rest, and can hold its breath for two hours. It probably dives over 3 kilometres (1.8 miles) deep to hunt for the squid and giant squid it enjoys eating.

Whale behaviour

- The humpback whale is the most acrobatic hunter. It "breaches" or leaps out of the water and dives with an enormous splash. The humpback also releases a "net" of bubbles to trap schools of fish. The fish cannot swim through the rising bubbles, and the humpback swims vertically up beneath them with its huge mouth wide open.

- The humpback is also a wonderful singer. It sings repeated notes and patterns, just like a bird. Some of the low, moaning noises it makes can be heard over 180 kilometres (112 miles) away. When humpbacks are alarmed, for example by the attack of killer whales, they can make a trumpeting noise of 170 decibels – louder than a jet engine.

- Whales migrate over huge distances, and are normally excellent navigators. Occasionally, though, whole groups of whales will run aground and end up dying on a beach. It is not known why this tragic event, called "stranding" happens.

59

DOLPHINS

Dolphins and porpoises are the smallest of the toothed whales. Their half-moon dorsal fin is sometimes mistaken for that of a shark, but they have a much friendlier nature. They are the acrobats of the whale family, leaping, somersaulting and spinning out of the water as if jumping for joy. They are magnificent swimmers, and will often "bowride" – finding the point at the bow of a passing boat where a pressure wave allows them to surf without swimming. Most dolphins hunt for fish and squid, though the enormous killer whale enjoys a much wider menu.

DOLPHINS
Dolphins swim in groups of up to 1,000 members. They hunt fish together like sheepdogs rounding up sheep, calling to each other with high-pitched shrieks and whistles. Dolphins on the coast of Laguna, Brazil, are famous for helping local fishermen by herding up red mullet and driving them towards their nets.

PORPOISE

Porpoises are the smallest of the whales. The vaquita porpoise weighs only 50 kilograms (110 pounds), and its name means "little cow". It is easy to tell the difference between a porpoise and a dolphin. Dolphins have a long thin jaw, giving them a distinctive "beak". Porpoises are more snub-nosed, which makes them look like mini whales.

KILLER WHALE

The killer whale, or orca, grows up to 10 metres (33 feet) long, three times bigger than most dolphins. The killer whale has beautiful black-and-white markings. The 2-metre (6½-feet) high triangular dorsal fin of the male is the biggest of any whale. The killer whale is the only whale with a taste for warm-blooded prey. It will feed on penguins, birds, seals, dugongs and other whales and dolphins. It will even attack the enormous blue whale. Killer whales hunt in well-organized packs, or "pods." They are well-named, because they are clever and ruthless hunters. Killer whales will bump into ice-floes to knock penguins into the water. They also surf onto beaches to catch seals sitting on the shore! One killer whale was found with the remains of 13 porpoises and 14 seals in its stomach.

Echolocation

• When dolphins and other toothed whales dive to catch fish, the water may be pitch-black, illuminated only by luminous fish, plankton, and ink squirted by squid. Instead of using their eyes, dolphins hunt in the same way as bats—with an advanced sonar system called echolocation. The dolphin uses the air beneath its blowhole to produce clicking sounds. It then shoots the sound waves forward through a lump of blubber in its forehead called the "melon." When the sound waves hit a fish, they bounce back as an echo. The dolphin's ear and brain are able to process all the echoes, and work out the distance and size of the object from which they rebounded. The human brain would struggle to recognize 20 clicks a second. But the dolphin can produce and analyze an amazing 700 clicks every second. The use of sound to recognize shapes is used by ships using sonar to detect submarines; and in ultrasound scans to examine unborn babies.

61

INDEX